THE PALACE

THE P

poems ANDE

ALACE

ÉS CERPA

ALICE JAMES BOOKS
New Gloucester, ME
alicejamesbooks.org

10 9 8 7 6 5 4 3 2 1

Alice James Books are published by Alice James Poetry Cooperative, Inc.

Alice James Books
Auburn Hall
60 Pineland Drive, Suite 206
New Gloucester, ME 04260
www.alicejamesbooks.org

Library of Congress Cataloging-in-Publication Data

Names: Cerpa, Andrés, 1990– author
Title: The palace / by Andrés Cerpa.
Identifiers: LCCN 2025024291 (print) | LCCN 2025024292 (ebook)
    ISBN 9781949944877 trade paperback | ISBN 9781949944754 epub
Subjects: LCGFT: Poetry
Classification: LCC PS3603.E747 P35 2026 (print) | LCC PS3603.E747 (ebook)
    DDC 811/.6—dc23/eng/20250610
LC record available at https://lccn.loc.gov/2025024291
LC ebook record available at https://lccn.loc.gov/2025024292

Alice James Books gratefully acknowledges support from individual donors,
private foundations, and the Poetry Foundation (https://www.poetryfoundation.org).

Cover photo by Jean Manuel Valentín

Contents

I

Late Work

I feel compelled to give you an ending, a promise of hope

to move against despair

even if the act is simple as falling in love, another city,

a long day casting shadows in the park.

I lost something & can't get over the fact—

the most powerful world

was the world of destruction & high. And/or,

I ran through the cane fields in splendor. When the interior

puzzled with the physical world

I cut myself down. The way & I became brothers.

Not blood. Not sugar. Not rust.

Snow in Calichoza.

In the too soon & always, I held the machete,

I built myself

a life.

You Must Live What You Don't Remember

The palace was never finished.

There was only time for labyrinth,

said the hounds.

We Are the Transient Ones

Too soon I became the thing that hunted & slept & slept

   alone. Devoid of ritual, & the apartment fathers up light.

Metaphor for the mind but still   *a heart of winter,*

               speedball, goodbye . . .

And why is it so hard to tell the truth about the past? What remains,

   almost untouched—

our time in the orchard where you became the orchard

      then laughed in a crevice of trees.

I feel the whispers of owls so far north that no human will ever see them again.

Memory is a dead animal lost in its grandeur. A wolf split & howling.

    A hawk as small as a leaf.

The Past

My mind cannot protect me here, at the green desk,
   where orcas blade the ocean like mountains

& the labyrinth is also the sky. The sky, where a thousand unnamed birds
   lift then dissolve into one.

     And so much has happened already—

for days, thinking the motion of men on pullup bars
     by the sea.

Streetlight. The night. Their rippled gleam
   framed by the waves & laughter . . .

A decade writing lines that were written.
     That week, that summer,

where I learned I needed to be alone on the steps & I was candle,
   an unnoticed gleam,

like the foil in the cigarette pack the pickpocket in my memory
   is touching, which makes me as real as the impossible likeness

of all things. In my 2014–2015 notebook—an untamed sketch of a church
   at the end of an alley, its secret beyond me

   as lavender blooms like a touch.

How can I return to the brief & motioned world? The lithe motion of the moon
   on the sea? And you, my past,

   reciting the lines as I read them—

Inferno. Visible breath. Impermanent address. The evening we walked to the skeletal
  horses the neighbors couldn't afford to feed anymore . . .

And a history in that debt. History—that mushroom cloud that dreams
  without a rider, that spurred & spurs us to sweep the torn villas

  as if bread was our one & only purpose.

I wanted things. So at the start of 7th grade I rode the ferry to Manhattan
  & asked for switchblades, butterfly knives, brass knuckles

  at the back of each shop.

The no's were clipped Newports. The no's felt like I'd never be enough.

Then midday on Centre Street, one shop owner locked the door.
  She lifted a black bag, all of it gleaming,

  onto the display. In reverence,

I chose each knife like the years as we lived them.
  Then sold them the next day at school.

The syllabus did not read, *You will live these moments forever,*
  you will write them down among trances of light

  you treated like pennies. You will wake in the woods with a dead cellphone & notebook,
  river water in your hair.

I need enough time to write the final poem, though it's all one poem,
  one orchard, one tree

in the forest of air.

There are no answers in death,
   but memory . . .

When I was a child, god held a blue butterfly knife
   to my jaw—

he begged me remember, he begged me
   to sing.

Some Eden

Uncle Charlie never called me at that time,
  & I never called him, or sent any money

as he moved through the veins of America,
  from Texas back to Tampa,

scratching at fleas. The success of his life,
  according to the dream—

he got out. And now, from this safety, I can romanticize
  his prayer book & even the fleas,

that stayed with him, from church basement to car to shelter,
  when really, somewhere in the gears,

between breath & the day the bank took his house,
  Tampa, where *he had it as good as he'd ever had it,*

became symbol, a glittering sea. In Texas, beneath a box fan
  in the shelter, without a diagnosis,

he prayed on it & knew. *Dumb luck
  that he even made it back.*

I don't call my first cousins, his children, & they are barely a blink
  in my day. But if history will have Uncle Charlie,

& I ask that it does,
  let us walk to a place where he is not the casualty

of something larger. We'd have to stand
  at the edge of a lava flow for that to happen—

a place where the earth makes new ground.

II

The Hounds

The labyrinth needs wings for its myth

  fair warning

& a soil to leave from.

Dear,

A fear of the poem is a fear of the future & I am afraid. At night, in the dark heirloom of the earth, I can feel the echo chamber of my failures, so I walk out of the bedroom, refill my water, smoke & look at my phone.

Then, the distrust of that time spent in the screen & no one to call hits me.

> Quote: *Like Larry said, 'Get your jacket & walk outside.'*

I can't remember the source, only the line, but the author is speaking of Levis, who wrote at night & died in Richmond, of an overdose, in a two-story home.

I am often thinned awake by visions of my father. Him, or signs of him.

Red shadow. Gray sleep.

> *Suicide is a decision to make no more decisions.*

I wander. It is summer & the city becomes sunshine & ether, a strange double exposure upon double exposure of life. My life.

In Washington Square Park, the mice dart from under the benches to feed in the open. They move from the safety of the earth to the nourishment of it &, for the most part, remain unnoticed.

Dramatic fractions govern the day.

I don't know you, so what should I say to the inexplicable future? A fear of the poem? A fear of the magic of the world results in purposeful distraction?

Where have they gone? My dead friends? My father? Where do we finally learn the afterlife or lack of it? Do ghosts thread dream catchers & avoid tears as best they can like us? Do they gamble? Do they drink? Do they sit in the parks they frequented in life?

Do they gather?

> *The best days of summer are the days of summer gone.*
> —Joe Bolton via Vallejo

Is that what I'm afraid of?

If bread is what god gave us as we wandered, & I find myself thinking about god more & more, then god only wanted us to wander (wonder) more.

Bread is not an answer.

> *If the horror of the world were the truth of the world,*
> *he said, there would be no one to say it*
> *& no one to say it to.*
> —Robert Hass quoting Basho

I am confused by how we fragment the world.

Afterlife? Empire? Song?

This life & no other.

I've watched the documentaries & it seems that migration is only another word for *unknown.*

We know where the whales travel,

but how do they know?

Wake Me in a Year

Until a hand reaches out from the fog—

 physical star

 in a frame of cold fire—

I drift. There doesn't need to be a word for every unnamed bird

 in flight.

Who knows where I am now?

Where do we meet?

Labyrinth after labyrinth,

 the hand.

When Did I Become So Vaguely Religious?

Even my body, pressed to the frost,

can make the beginnings of spring.

Delphi

The horses starved then came back as snow,

dementia, fire, rings in the trees

swaddling frost. For a year,

sparse meals & our child in mud.

This morning, I worried about money,

the life we've made & the future,

how long it would take to dig out the car.

I left my job for visions of horses—

I'm never coming back

was the lie. Debt. Rent. A child.

At the center of the world,

our hands in a blizzard of touch.

Heroin

Inside the glimmer

there is a current of cold smoke

that prisms.

Yes, death makes us visible, makes lace

a refusal

to die.

But I am all the ghosts tending the soil

& waiting to hold you. Just this once,

fuck a euphemism,

I'll demystify my presence—

I am no moon,

(your dead friends stay dead)

no metaphor

for light.

Works Cited

From the plane, I watch clouds over the country

 as a thin cup of coffee trembles on a tray.

The world is not dead

 & my hair grows

longer. With gloves,

 an agent images

my hands. I am guided to a room.

 I am ordered to sit

beneath a clock. Like a mountain,

 an agent reads

 every page of every book

I have carried.

 I wait.

He pins moths to the walls

 of my sleep. Autumn

ensues. Something irrevocable

 has happened.

Diaspora Poem

And in the dream, there were attempts at reconciliation,

  houses foreclosed

& a library, empty of students,

  collapsed in miniature

onto my lap. I wanted. I wanted

  a home, the sea & the orchard, to be tucked away

in a blue envelope

  with care. In the fierce tremble

of hoof-light & fog,

  myth & fact at once—

I am/was a thief & addict. In this country,

  heaven is a memory I can't touch.

Fog in the Mouth of the Mountain

There is a feeling within me I can't touch

that reminds me of a heaven ascending,

an always autumn where the sunset lingers

in a cash-for-gold like splendor.

And today I am alive by a thread—a road that ends

with my friends opening their arms,

the mountains beneath them,

as they say simple things like *It's good to see you.*

It's been too long. How was the drive?

The Most Honest Poem I Could Write Today

The trees are magnificent & the rain woke me
from a dream about treading water
in the dark. I called my Grandma last week.
It was her birthday & she asked Jesus to help her
die. I tried to divert her from death & religion
but she is 85 (we counted) & sad.
I am 33 & always losing my phone.
I worry that the drugs & concussions
+ the family's medical history
have done or are doing their work. Despite all that
& the thing about my losing phone,
I remember being 17 at the edge of a pond
at the edge of a forest
as a city of fireflies began to emerge.
How can that one moment of awe, which feels like the quiet opposite
of what is happening to my brain,
last longer than so many things? Most days
are like typing variations of the same password
in the same room of forgiveness & sky.
My mind is turning toward money, but I'm going to divert that
for as long as I can.
My wife & I are having a child.
I want to be there, but because I can change the rain to snow
I'm afraid my mind will vanish too soon.
That the gift of concussions & the dead people I love
will pull me away.
The wolves are a symbol.
I am confused by the labyrinth of this book.
I was popping open a floorboard with a butterfly knife
when the sun shone on my 8th grade graduation.
This is more a sketch of a poem than a poem
because I woke with the line, *When I die, my stories will die*
with me, then carved those words into my desk.
They won't accept it if it's too psychedelic or religious,

read a poem I read before writing this poem.

But my books don't sell, so I have the luxury of writing what I want.

Anyways, I trust you enough to know you'll forgive me at my word

when I say all those psychedelic & religious moments mattered deeply.

I read *Death Comes to the Archbishop* then lent it to my mom,

forgetting the marginalia at the end of Chapter 1.

Ha! I say the same thing about psychedelic drugs.

And now for another reject scene I've been waiting to tell you:

In 2020, I was working the Census after I was laid off by the university.

My supervisor's name was J.R. His band, The Royal Hounds,

stopped touring in March.

The job was to enumerate beach towns in New Jersey.

Houses that hadn't answered via online or post.

As we walked from 10 people living in a two-bedroom apartment

to Escalades & infinity pools,

we talked about empty desks, the appeal of the ocean & music.

We are paupers in the kingdom,

he said, while we were eating peanut butter sandwiches on a curb.

I'd like to say I'll never forget that moment

but maybe I will. *When I die,*

my stories will die with me.

But at least I wrote this book.

III

In Locust & Wild Honey

For money, for bread, corridor by corridor,

 we swept the torn villas. To suffer the less,

we left. We suffered.

Diaspora Poem

The dead rise in me—

their three gold teeth like distant armies

in the dusk.

Abuela is among them.

She hauls a cart that drips the first horse's blood.

My husband was haunted

she tongues. *I did not protect the second child,*

but saved what little I could

for you & your sister's

college.

You will not smell this death wish,

overflowing

through the trees. Or return

to the mountain of your birth.

Adolescence

I'll enter heaven holding my sins

like a knife in a North Face coat.

Diaspora Poem

The past holds forever larger space
in the mind.
Example: She is dead but I'm playing dominoes with my Abuela in her kitchen
when she loses the past tense
completely. The Section 8 bars are a precise & rusted script,
a labyrinth that frames the weathered flag of Puerto Rico
as she describes the tortured parrot that the professor at U.P.R.
who asked her, *What do you want to study?*
keeps in his office. He must be dead now too, but his question lives like one blue falling
as the animal, again, rips at its wings. *I don't know.*
I don't know why I'm visiting. I can't leave
my father at home. Abuela says, *Andrés, they are offering me a scholarship.*
But we, Sister Maria & Mami & me, rushed home
after his questions. Abuela was proud that I studied in a different state,
that I majored in English, that soon,
I, like my father, would hold a degree.
We didn't come to this country to starve.
We came here to study & eat.

The Years as We Lived Them

after Li-Young Lee

Like pushing a grocery cart home because the car won't start

or watching *Law & Order* in a laundromat,

the repetition & starlight beyond the dimming interiors of two-story homes,

mixed with the fact of the universe expanding,

creates a feeling like chalkboards

erased in a dream. As I write this,

the leaves with a darkness that gives. The things I couldn't afford

but wanted because I was trying to fulfill a photograph, old,

of my grandfather in his hometown in 1966—a river, a machete, a family, a car—

returning in grandeur with a Rolex

from the States. If failure follows a greed fevered script, I have failed.

I work & worry. I take 200 mg once a day.

It was my 31st birthday & she was wearing her coat in the kitchen—a failure—

when she suggested we walk to the library.

I wrote a poem as she read.

We cut home through the park.

Her eyes like honeyed lanterns

in the dark.

I Learned to Ride a Bicycle in Silver Lake Park

The room felt like loosening teeth
when I lifted myself from the bed.
Rain. Summer. Making coffee in the dark.
Touching the window felt like being outside
a bubble of lamplight
in Silver Lake Park. Or being in a painting
of Silver Lake Park. Decades returning.
Searching my father's last words
for a map.

The Map

There was no applause when god entered the labyrinth, carrying a dead man

  as an example

      by his throat. There were birds & lathework

but the people that tended its growth had gone home to their corner

      encampments.

To watch your children go gaunt. To be conquered. To be blindfolded by history

      & asked to lead the way.

Hunger is a teacher,

      god said. *It masters even time.* For when hunger became the forest became

         a cacophony of voices,

& every hoofprint & drift became us,

      alert.

In hunger, being alive was being alive for each & every cell. The labyrinth is a cell.

      North, & I kept running—

Abuela died in the Bronx with a gold-plated cross

      on her neck.

I ran through the woods with a gold-plated cross

      on my neck.

IV

I Am Every Bomb in My Safety

I'm trying to grieve the death of my father, my overdosed friends,
  stay clean, raise a child,

      buy a house—

I once thought, *No political poems.*

      I'll knife the subject

      we're trying to survive.

Rent

We buried the dog. No tomb but a rock to protect it.

A rock like a 9 pm cloud. A secret. A trespass.

What a beautiful place to sleep.

Beyond the Poem

for James Baldwin

France in lavender

outside the city walls. If we walk

arm in arm

long enough . . .

Two Coffins

In the beach towns of heaven,

I was lighting a spliff

in the sun. The archive—

a watch & a wolfskin coat

stitched with letters.

When I die,

my stories will die

with me.

Machete

I am more than the world you asked me to be—

tributary dissolving the brain,

sediment like Fentanyl

in the vein. Clean needle. The alley,

the first valley, the diasporic dream—

your hands become earth

then rise as a tricked-out Jeep,

a ghost horse

tethered to the fender.

Now, I am pen.

I am after. Before snow,

I traded yucca for ether

& had no need for a coat.

The Now Is So Ancient It Hurts

Will I be 17 on a rooftop forever?

   Blunted. Drunk. Near death

in the snow?

Slow Projection

The stock market falls. I contribute to my pension.

And what do the rotations mean

as we mean them?

What can I hold?

In bed last night,

I woke to the nightmare again. Not repeating dream

but the dream

of their hunger. Two open hands.

The child asks for bread in the snow dance

& the trains continue to run.

V

We Will Not Be Forgiven Our Careless Lives

I woke only once

among the shepherds

painting the stones

with their lips.

Elegy with Atlantic City in All Its Glory

I ride with whatever the dream tells me

until I'm double exposure,

sinned out & hungry,

eye-to-eye with the aftermath

of the text—

a hush like cards on felt

when I'm losing

& far past the plan

where this blackjack table is gonna build me a temple

with a two-car garage.

At the end of the end of the morning,

I don't mind that I lost. The glittering Escalade

of American wealth is screaming its silence,

while M., an old friend,

sleeps in the hull of a plane.

The dirt bike he paid for by cleaning casinos in college

is now in his mother's garage. Ten years ago,

the government called me up

when he needed security clearance,

because they interview everyone you'd ever known

to never know anyone

again. I slip into story

the way a pill slips into the system—

heavy marketing & an algorithm

of air.

And though I've never won much at cards

or had me a job enough

to make me a carbon fiber frame

in the belly of the market

as it falls,

I've put plenty of money on the table,

plastic in the ocean

& forgone the indictment

of my speech.

This is the story

with sticks of dynamite in a whale,

the lullaby of children burning trash to generate heat

as a couple hundred horses fuse

to fly in a make-believe heaven,

then come down

because commercials & sweat.

I didn't want to make M. feel like he was radioactive

when he sat next to me

draped in an American flag. I wanted to place him

somewhere else.

On the 6th grade trip to Washington D.C.,

I touched the black wall

& was moved.

It should be easier to talk about the future

with a ghost. But what happens when that ghost shot-gunned

a few beers in the shower, & knew you when you were 18,

& moves through the years talking football & karate,

dirt bikes & pills? Fuck the American flag,

but I didn't want to make M. feel radioactive

or incur the indictment of my speech.

North,

or I am already buried

in my childhood awe, in auburn & the potential

of fire.
                I held my slingshot,

barefoot in the dappling light

& heard a river, stone after stone,

until the pine bed hovered,

I hovered,

still.

      ~

If I could choose my own story—

the conifers of heaven

would exist in my chest.

But every mattress dollar

my wife & I save

never seems to be enough.

A little land. A place

where the child, wild with laughter,

feels safe?

From the Beach at Night

Storm-worn houses

bank the narrow streets

while three beers smoke

at the table.

A chair for me,

saved.

I will die in this country

to be close to my friends.

Then a Humpback Breaks from the Surface

I feel kind & kinda beautiful now

after a day of rain in the cottage.

So still, not even (   ) could interrupt.

~

I have still made space for (   ).

Repeated the form of despite.

~

But let's make a cento together,

by knifing out every (   ) in this book,

every unlearned splendor

& noose.

~

Rain today. The whales. Good boots.

VI

Self-Portrait at 34

And the shimmer of the lake as I hiked alongside it, through pine bed & dusk,

the first time I took LSD,

remains the anchor of a time when every slow movement

drew from a well

that still runneth over my cup—

Colin twisting a 40 oz in Tompkins Square Park, Devon on a rooftop,

slingshots, knives, basketball practice, & all those long days falling into myself

as I was & would become, connect & connect,

until I am holding my child by a river,

stunned by the shimmer I share with my wife

& how all those soft diamonds on the water are my youth & also now.

Then the cool breath of debris—branches, leaves in the shallows

going soft. What a joy to been woven

into the pattern—

my face disappearing like the face disappearing

on a $100 bill. The power & slow slip of my body,

this held breath like clouds, & my silence fighting memory's silence like the day I held my father's last voicemail

over the child's crib.

Going further into the water was like winding a watch

to a time when Abuela would bring her yellowed kitchen to the park—

the pots, the oil, & the memory

of eating beneath trees as she storied how the trade winds

would throw sand from the Sahara onto her porch,

that even in the mountains her mother would sweep sand . . .

If I were to continue into the gloaming of soft diamonds,

what would I remember?

It is a dangerous joy to remember.

Then a Voice to Remember This Heaven

Some days are simple enough—

Right now, there is pastel in the sky & I have health insurance.

I just finished a long run

on the beach. The windows of my car are open

& I am sweating

in the breeze. Taking off my shoes, taking off my socks,

I feel the salt

of what's left over. Waves of panic

drowned.

Some days are simple enough—

Barefoot, leaning into the cool metal of my own car,

staring at the sky & drinking water . . .

It's so simple

—my voice breaks a bit in the recording—

I could cry.

Late Work

A fear of the poem is a fear of the future & I am afraid.

In the dark heirloom of the earth, I was nourished.

 Am nourished.

I question god.   The country's ugly gossamer

 weaves another dusk. The horizon in starved horses.

Everything all at once.

As we walk,

 I hold the secret vein: my child: an emerald

 in the heirloom of the earth.

Poem

I was watching her watching me

drink a beer under a mountain & wanting all the years back

seemed foolish.

The meal tasted like earth

& clean water.

The sun shower so gentle & slow

we didn't even flinch—

what luck that I was changed.

Shield

for Franz Wright

Here, wherever here is, is
  the real world.

. . . night trees . . .

A leaf falls to my hands
  like a shield.

Phantom Cart

When my wife & child are asleep, I smoke outside in my coat,

  shirtless beneath, in an earlier blue. The past

is not the past

  if I can hold it. Yet my child,

who will not remain *my child*

  but a realness unto herself,

might lullaby or eulogy or despise these poems

  in a future gesture toward myth.

I cannot ask for forgiveness this early.

  In the frame,

in the parameters of law,

  no angel comes down to protect her.

Vile magic or *Vile magic we are.*

  Maybe a little snow will come down

in the dance.

  Looks like it.

I have placed her mittens on the table & showered away the smoke.

In a Country

And when the rains came
 like lean wolves

we were ready. The statues strewn with purpose,
 half-buried in myth,

in the fecund already
 filling with color

like the last practice of a dance that stretched like honeysuckle
 on the border of a marble quarry,

where a girl, enslaved, leaned to test the taste of a flower

& imagined her name imprinted
 on the road to the temple at Delphi,

so that there was no doubt, not ever,
 of her freedom.

        ~

Her name in an earth screaming,
 Debt & torches & sharks.

        ~

North—

& a thousand horses pull through the dream of a little land
& I must feed them

    more

than stories & touch.

~

Ghosts, not stars,
on the flag.

~

It is beginning to snow in the mind

& I am digging out the car, that rust-stained 120,000 miles of dream,

returning where I've woken,
 gift after gift,

thankful & bruised

as the faint music of the past opens
 like a snarl—

the clarity of nests abandoned by winter, the apartment, the cathedrals of youth

where swallows in the last feed ate the sky
 of foreign cities

        as I smoked.

~

The yard is a half-finished altar,
 a rat's nest of tears.

~

Carved into the ether, the day
  god gave me a knife.

    ~

Bombs & the muffled screams of the dead.

    ~

There is no land, no palace,
  or money for rent.

To hold onto these dreams—horses at the trough, consuming the fire
  in gulps.

And my child at the door, in a bright purple coat,

tying her boots
  as I start up the car.

    ~

I am here & also sitting in a fortress
  by the sea.

I am here in the dream of the land, in the sky I was given
  & give to my child

in paused moments of warmth—

    ~

Also this . . .

~

A kite lost in the grave-clouds,
 & her birthday next week.

~

Also this . . .

~

The snows never came back
 to hide us. Wolves in the labyrinth, guarded by guards

that shoot down any leaving
 from their posts.

~

And the dog we buried in ceremony, in a beach towel,

as we decided an afterlife, a heaven in miniature, a now,

where her dog & grandfather
are never alone

& I imagine, alone, in the moment she crosses the threshold & sticks out her tongue,
 the part of story where she can visit this place in the future,

because we own the land, & can afford to keep everything as it was.

~

I place the shovel in the trunk.

~

In a country we've built another country, a home,
 though it's mostly a poem, a story

before bed—

there is good water to drink
 & horses,

 wolves & dangers

in the ways we can explain
 & prepare for.

The road to this country is a thread.

A benevolent fire.

~

Imagine it with me.

Step in. Let us in.

Ghost Flag, Hours, Open Map

Then one night I became the knife

the tree swallowed—

an heirloom, a century

of leaving the wound

& wounded alone.

The ancestors made, killed,

then half-buried me in green,

in the secret

rings, my blue handle

exposed to the world.

Now, I am swaddled

& final. From their movement,

a scar—everyone I love

is here.

VII

Knives & Winter & Pills

I will need a thousand springs to forget the old language.

  (I love the old language)

I will live a thousand springs.

Notes & Acknowledgments

"We Are the Transient Ones" takes its title from an unpublished poem by Franz Wright. I discovered this line through Bianca Giaever's catalog, *Two Years with Franz Wright* (Transom, 2018). In addition, the poem borrows the line "And why is it so hard to tell the truth about the past?" from Joe Bolton's poem "The Changes." The poem can be found in *The Last Nostalgia: Poems 1982-1990* (University of Arkansas Press, 1999).

"Dear," contains language from Joe Bolton's translation of passages from César Vallejo's *Trilce*, Charles Wright's elegy to Larry Levis, and Robert Hass's poem "Winged & Acid Dark."

"Heroin" is inspired by Franz Wright's poem "Alcohol."

"Works Cited" is inspired by the poetry of W.S. Merwin and Solmaz Sharif.

"Fog in the Mouth of the Mountain" is for my friends Stef and Tyler. Thanks, homies.

"The Most Honest Poem I Could Write Today" contains language from David Berman's "Self-Portrait at 28." The poem is for my friend and 2020 Census manager, J.R.

The title of "The Years as We Lived Them" emerged from Li-Young Lee's poem "Braiding" which reads, "How I wish we didn't hate those years while we lived them."

"Elegy with Atlantic City in All its Glory" is inspired by Mark Jarmon's poem "Ground Swell."

"Self-Portrait at 34" is inspired by David Berman's "Self-Portrait at 28."

"In a Country" takes its title from a Larry Levis poem of the same name.

Eternal gratitude to Lorainne Hanseberry, Larry Levis, Joe Bolton, Ruth Ellen Kocher, Daniel Alarcón, Franz Wright, and David Berman. Your work helped me find my way.

Thank you to the editors, staff, and artists that believed in these in poems.

Poems from *The Palace* were previously published in *Virginia Quarterly Review*, *Ploughshares*, *The Journal*, *The Rumpus*, *Huizache*, and VONK's album, *A songbook of rare feelings*.

Thank you to the Randolph College MFA community. Your spirit encouraged me.

Thank you to Rigoberto González, maestro, who has nurtured me and so many other artists.

Thank you to my daughter for the joy she brings into our home.

And most of all, thank you to my wife for her enduring support and love.

Recent Titles from Alice James Books

Let the Moon Wobble, Ally Ang

The Seeds, Cecily Parks

All the Possible Bodies, Iain Haley Pollock

Saint Consequence, Michael M. Weinstein

Freeland, Leigh Sugar

Mothersalt, Mia Ayumi Malhotra

When the Horses, Mary Helen Callier

Cold Thief Place, Esther Lin

If Nothing, Matthew Nienow

Zombie Vomit Mad Libs, Duy Đoàn

The Holy & Broken Bliss, Alicia Ostriker

Wish Ave, Alessandra Lynch

Autobiomythography of, Ayokunle Falomo

Old Stranger: Poems, Joan Larkin

I Don't Want To Be Understood, Joshua Jennifer Espinoza

Canandaigua, Donald Revell

In the Days That Followed, Kevin Goodan

Light Me Down: The New & Collected Poems of Jean Valentine, Jean Valentine

Song of My Softening, Omotara James

Theophanies, Sarah Ghazal Ali

Orders of Service, Willie Lee Kinard III

The Dead Peasant's Handbook, Brian Turner

The Goodbye World Poem, Brian Turner

The Wild Delight of Wild Things, Brian Turner

I Am the Most Dangerous Thing, Candace Williams

Burning Like Her Own Planet, Vandana Khanna

Standing in the Forest of Being Alive, Katie Farris

Feast, Ina Cariño

Decade of the Brain: Poems, Janine Joseph

American Treasure, Jill McDonough

We Borrowed Gentleness, J. Estanislao Lopez

Brother Sleep, Aldo Amparán

Sugar Work, Katie Marya

Museum of Objects Burned by the Souls in Purgatory, Jeffrey Thomson